MW01253615

# Rack of Lamb

## Michael Kenyon

Brick Books

CANADIAN CATALOGUING IN PUBLICATION DATA

Kenyon, Michael.
  Rack of lamb

Poems.
ISBN 0-919626-48-3

I. Title.

PS8571.E59R32 1991   C811'.54   C91-093108-9
PR9199.3.K46R32 1991

Brick Books gratefully acknowledges the assistance of
The Canada Council and the Ontario Arts Council.

The author thanks Marlene Cookshaw, Marnie Parsons
and Sue Schenk.

Typeset in Ehrhardt and printed on Zephyr Antique laid.
Sewn into signatures and bound by The Porcupine's Quill.

Brick Books
Box 38
Station B
London, Ontario
N6A 4V3

This book is for Muriel and Tom.

I think of it as melodious, softening the noises of the knives and forks, not dominating them, not imposing itself. It would fill up those heavy silences that sometimes fall between friends dining together.   *Erik Satie*

Soon the dam will be completed. It is an immense wall that will seal off the valley from one mountain to the other, creating a lake more than five miles around. We will have to vacate our home to make room for it.   *Ibuse Masuji*

# PEPPERS

## Peppers

Any day you can go out the door and meet somebody and change your life. Mary please this minute leave what you're doing, fetch Angelina with the long nails to come peel peppers. That's how I feel today, everything is clear and each thing different. Don't slam the door, child!

Last night I dreamed of going to the doctor's to get my stitches out. I've half a year's birth control pills left, seems such a waste, you know? So in the dream I ask could he maybe give them to someone? Weirdest dream.

Well let's see, he says. Didn't you open any?

No, I say, why should I?

Look! he says. And he peels back the foil from each pack and shows me, one after another, these real cute arrangements of candies: licorice allsorts, jelly beans, dark chocolates.

Angelina's coming, good, I hope you told her right away, not next week. Take those gulls, now. Three gulls all the same you think but look close, take your time with each one, make your mind a picture, no, a movie, because they fly and you follow, one at a time, all different. Turn the peppers will you Bruno? Yes of course they're hot, use the stick, all right the mittens if you like, but don't burn them on the element. I love the smell, kind of smoky, kind of sharp – for heaven's sake pull out the rack Bruno, don't reach in like that. So anyway, you never know when you're gonna walk down the street and meet somebody very important. Where is that girl? They should be black, black like scorched, all over. And maybe it's somebody you already know, someone you've known for a long time, maybe your whole life. I don't say it's likely, but you got to admit it's possible.

## Fiddlehead Greens

Sometimes at night I stand in the living room and twitch open the drapes and stare down at the trees rising from the valley. Let my eyes follow the highway, the lines of headlights leading through the dark, and imagine I'm leaving. Last year I fell in love with a Mormon missionary and went to Salt Lake City and watched slide shows for a week. I was baptized in a swimming pool. I had an underwater vision. I saw a tree whose leaves turned into birds, the flock of birds flew away in the shape of a tree. I couldn't look at anyone afterward, not even the man I thought I was in love with. The first person I made eye contact with was a floor girl in Safeway fruit and vegetables. She had the most beautiful translucent skin I've ever seen. I copied her name from the tag she wore – I would pretend she was a distant cousin, so I could save her. Sometimes when I stare out I get very frightened, I say to myself over and over, *Gone mad with foreboding, gone mad with foreboding –* I read it in *Reader's Digest* once – *gone mad with foreboding,* till the words seem completely strange.

# Tomatoes

I eat in this room in this chair. Always. I eat alone, not with people. Always. Oblong tomatoes are perfect in this kind of sauce but they're not in season right now, not in my garden I should say, and when I zipped down to the supermarket I couldn't bring myself to buy anything except a bag of these little cherry jobs – no good for cooking, so the sauce is a bit pale. I'm not over the moon about regular-size or giants raw, but tomato cherries, they're OK. Little splashes of colour in your mouth. I close my eyes and bite and get yellow-red-green all at once. Surprise, surprise! I've tried to catch my face in the TV screen but it won't work with eyes open. I just see me chewing – stupid, which is why I don't eat with anyone, stupid is why I turn on the box. Go ahead, try one. You ever imagine such a big TV? I never. You better believe it cost a bundle.

When I eat I travel in space and time. New Zealand fifty million years ago. You think that's crazy? Seems long ago and far away to you? Listen. Channel nine. Hey, you gonna stand there you may as well stir. Listen. I'm talking about no people here. Peaceful, huh? Just the noodles coming to boil. The lake out there's bigger than it looks. I eat good, I fix my breakfast lunch and dinner. Spaghetti, homemade sauce, tomato cherries, alfalfa sprouts. My sister's boyfriend was called Alf, sometimes I think that word might go on forever, alfalfalfalf, good grief! Preparation, you asking about preparation? Nothing to it. Standing in the kitchen fifty million years.

Hey, you see that lake out there? My sister drowned in it, yeah really, in the lake in the summer, drowned. Took the divers five days to find her. Used to be I couldn't get the time right, cold spaghetti and spicy sauce stuck to the bottom of the pan. Heck, I don't mind watching folks eat, that's entertaining. But don't you reckon I'll ever leave this house, I mean move away, you hear?

Think I'll die in this house. Jesus, that's not morbid, that's beautiful! I love my sister, you see? Look at that surface, quiet and still. Yeah. You think I'm unhappy by myself in the country, you're wrong. No, I'm not going to start till you leave, I can wait long as it takes. Sometimes I stare out and stare out, won't be the first time I've eaten cold. The sun shines, the wind blows, all the ducks are flying home.

## Kibbles

I was a girl again! Late Tuesday night doing needlepoint, Pooch was asleep in front of the fire, George in the garage with his train set, I look up from my work and there are snowflakes whirling outside the window, like peace and happiness trying to get in, all of a sudden I remember the leaning snow fence, the shadows ripply on the drifted snow, the bungalow all new-painted white with bright red shutters and lace sheers. I was a girl again, it was just lovely. Pooch opened his eyes without lifting his head and looked at me, thumped his tail real slow and dreamy.

# Lemon Loaf

One early morning in spring a year or two after we built this house I looked out from my room into the garden and saw no less than five cougars playing. The biggest drank from the fountain, while the others frolicked in the marrow patch over there behind the trellises. Not a very fitting word for cougars, frolicked, but that's what they did. Such a paradise this garden, don't you think? A hundred years ago not a white person in miles. My late husband used often to remark on that. My bedroom is the top window on the left, you should see the view, the forests are such a green this time of year. Every winter I appreciate green a little more. Shall I be mother?

Now I'm alone I go to sleep at night thinking as I sleep the world changes – tomorrow when I wake up everything will be different. I'm disturbed before dawn by strange noises. Every morning I imagine I'm seeing the earth as God intended.

It's chilly when the sun begins to dip, don't you find? Let's go inside. Do say yes. I've had a fire lit in my room, you can get warm before you leave, I can show you the view. You're lucky you came at this season, because the blossoms have only begun to open and you can still see through the fruit trees the barest sliver of sea on the horizon. The sea and horizon and forests disappear from April to October. In a wind the blossoms blow like hail against my window. You're surely not concerned? It isn't really a bedroom, more a kind of suite. I have my library and my favourite chair, and if I open the window, the room fills with the scent.

# Couscous

Watch my lips when I say it. Erotic, no? More sexy than caviar, I believe, but it should be steamed over meaty broth, here they just pour on boiling water. Hello, Yvonne! Hello, Charles! Ça va? The last thing I did with my body was in Kenya. I had to take off my dress so many times I lost count. By the end it seemed silly. When I saw the rushes I couldn't believe the giraffes, zebras, rhinos, elephants, those flesh-tearing birds, I forget the name, and the jungle, the plains. Look, there's Francis, d'you know Francis? He's very sympathetic, but strictly dull dull dull. Where was I?

Ah, Africa. Victoria Falls roaring beside my big lovely face, the director gave me a nightlight just like it. Well poppy, sugarheart, of course I know the Falls is not in Kenya. It was some other falls. Isn't it a wonderful party? My roles after? Yes, you would ask that. They were poor affairs, I was past thirty, I couldn't take the closeup anymore. A dreadful time in my life.

But Africa, I'll tell you about Africa if you promise not to laugh. Promise? I was at my peak in that film, my face and body were superb, you would not believe how beautiful. I played in every scene, almost every shot, I never used a stand-in. Everyone desired me, the black extras, the crew, even the other women. I watched the rushes over and over. Mon ami, I stared so hard I started to imagine I had something that other women lacked, something tender, sensitive, not physical like a dimple or eyebrows, but deeper, more mysterious. I sat in the dark and looked at that goddess in *National Geographic* nature and *Vogue* clothes, and I knew – sugarheart, your face! I'm teasing you. I'm drunk. Quelle horreur! You are too serious, you're a choirboy.

# Roast Duck

The city is too full of tricks. That's why we got this place, it's kind of in the country. I don't mind working nights, I just don't want to talk about it. The cops came yesterday, woke me up, said if there was blood on the carpet it might be Nadine's. They took the door mat, for Christ's sake, so I had to buy another. I got one that says WELCOME. Billy went nuts, barking all round them, they said he should wear a muzzle. Assholes.

God I hate uniforms.

I went: Maybe Nadine came in with her date? Maybe he squeezed his fingers round her neck? Maybe there was no shank? I went: You figure it out, I gotta set the dining table, I'm expecting guests.

The greasy cops were flapping notebooks against their thighs, trying to stay cool.

Word on the street is Nadine's been offed. She was Larry's people same as me and I want to know where the fuck he was. Checking out new merchandise is a good bet. I told her never to bring a date here, to our house – now *he* knows where I live, so do the cops. Four hundred a night last four nights, doesn't help my sleep.

When Larry comes over I give him a hug and a kiss, but it's like putting my mouth to a mirror. I go, What's wrong?

Jesus fuck! goes Larry. But he's not square, man, he does me good. We stand in the room, loosen up some.

The WELCOME has disappeared. Instead there's a window the size of the mat. Like someone has put a window in the carpet. Like we're in a glass-bottom boat. Below is the scene, the exact same wet night street I stand on every bar rush. Big Tammy bending into a glittering Mercedes. Every few seconds she wiggles her silver bum. Horns play scales behind the stopped car.

There's this old guy alone on the corner; the guy looks scared, he squints up, the skylight must be in his eyes, but I don't know how to turn it down. Working girls don't notice a thing. They got yellow umbrellas, they hunch over cigarettes on the sidewalk. A hooker in the rain blows steam from her nostrils. Leather straps round her legs. A flock of starlings like herring I caught when I was a kid flies from City Hall to the shops; when the Mercedes makes a second pass they come soaring up, through the welcome mat and into the room.

Me and Larry shield our faces and there's Nadine standing real straight in the dark wind. I scream at her. Man, I scream.

# Onion

Who're you? I don't give a damn. Where's my sherry? I don't know, I guess I don't have any. Can't stop shaking, honest to God, it's bad, bad. You don't understand what it's like, do you? I can tell. Morrie? I know, I know, I was just thinking. Get me some Brights, will you? get me some. Where you going? Oh, onions. Get 'em from the corner, don't have to tell you that. You looking at me funny? Got something to say, say it. I paid you already, we're all square. This is my place, my house, I got a right to say what I think in my own place. Better watch it, I'm a crazy bitch. I'm sorry, sorry. You're a good boy. You remind me of my grandson, got just his way of talking, 'course he's university, you university? I can tell. Maybe in the basement. Maybe there.

Haven't been down in a long time. Probably no good, though, grow them long green tails and go soft, rotten in the end. What you need them for anyway? You're coming back, ain't you? Get me a pack of smokes, I don't care about the fucking doctor. Get me –

What? Oh, Players. Players. You will come back? You said – I'm not really hungry. I haven't any money, yeah it was in the drawer, I know, I don't know what happened. Maybe it got stolen. I don't think I've got any. That cheque, remember? No, that was some- one else. Who're you? You been before, ain't you? Bullshit. Liar. Think because I, think I can't remember a face I seen, because I really don't – I'm all messed up, all messed up. Don't leave me. My worker, the other one, nobody ever made soup, from scratch. Oh, Jesus! No, I'm all right, don't worry about me, I'm not worth the time. I used to make it, not from a packet, when my kids was little, just a gas pain, it'll go away, if I could only stop this bloody shaking. I give you the key, didn't I? You lock the door after. I won't be a bad girl, nobody can't, if you care about, that's why I. Oh shit. Morrie? is that you Morrie? It's all falling out. You won't forget the smokes, will you sweetheart?

## Dill Pickles

I remember Bob whistling in time to his footsteps as he climbed the stairs. Mozart. I stood here, furious, and watched a jay steal a silk scarf from the line – dark blue, a streaming banner.

Look at the faded upholstery, used to be so bright. The leaf pattern on the curtains also. These are my things. If I close my eyes and take a deep breath, everything fits. The velvet leaves still billow from the window. I can't tell by touching whether the pile has gone or if it's just my old fingers. Some rooms on the ground floor have been boarded up for nearly fifteen years. Before he died, Bob nailed shutters over the windows of the rooms we never used.

I often go down and stare at the heaps of junk, thinking to find something. Last time I saw the glint of a jar, a big pickler, over by the front window. Behind it a crack of buttery daylight through a split board. Not much of a discovery, was it? But it belongs. This year I'll clear a patch in the weeds out there and plant cucumbers. I'll make them grow in the shadow under the jay's flight, the place so difficult to fill in.

## Spaghetti Bolognese

Everything's lousy, thanks for asking. Last night I went to see the alderman. Knocked on his door and told him I wanted to know where he stood on the dam. You can have ten minutes, he said. So he spouts ten minutes of tight-lipped bullshit. Hungry? he said. Always, I said, gave him a smile. He said, OK, you open the wine.

He said Hello when we met, Good night when he turned out the light, Good morning in the morning. Before sleep he read to me from a psych text called *An Introduction to the Family*.

He's pompous, my God, he didn't even believe the reason for my visit, just assumed I wanted to sleep with him.

I said, You don't care about flooding the valley?

He said, Of course I care about flooding the valley.

Anyhow, it's beautiful. A big crystal hanging between the fridge and stove. Sun comes through the window, paints rainbows on the wall. This morning when he left for the city I fixed myself a sandwich, snooped around. He's got *A History of Europe* upside down with his cookbooks, an old highway sign that says Grand Coulee....

Jesus. OK, I don't know what it means. What about you? You live here. What've you got? Your own cookbooks? Nobody knows much.

I feel more and more nervous. We need information so we can act, right? My foot's gone to sleep. My whole leg has stars in it.

# *Coffee*

God, I feel terrific, I can't believe it, I see him again this evening, he wants us to meet every day. It's happened so fast. Wham. Something I can't stop and it changes everything, the whole world. He's gentle. He's smart too. Doesn't matter that he's rich. I just think about him all the time. I fly to work, fly home, the LAWNS look different. I don't notice the rain till I find my umbrella wide open in the bathtub next day. I keep remembering stuff from when I was a kid, Sundays in church, wet coats, mystery and such. Honestly, I'm waiting with my whole body. You know how wonderful slow minutes are? vanishing nights? But you're a guy, maybe it's not the same for you. Pretty silly, I guess, more coffee? I'm not drinking coffee at the moment, when we first met at the restaurant I thought it was the coffee, I'm stupid that way. I shouldn't be admitting this. I've got no perspective. We're living on salads. I tremble whenever I look at him. He's lovely and I can't believe he wants to see me every day and TIME OUT I want to shout TIME OUT let me get my breath let me get my arms round this

# Gingerbread

You're not watching! You gotta watch! We'll do it again. Ready? Ready? You chop first. OK. Go! The first axe comes through the door, a baby dies, and daddy runs away. The second axe comes through the door, a baby dies, and mommy runs away. The third axe comes through the door, a baby dies, and – this is the hard part –

# Soyburgers

It's very easy. You can use just soybeans, or any combination of dry beans. I used a cup of soybeans and a cup each of mung and chickpeas. You could substitute split peas or lentils for the mung. Anything you want, really. Add at least twice the amount of water and simmer for maybe four hours (soak the beans overnight to

reduce the cooking time) – they have to be nice and soft. OK. Then you mash two cups of the drained cooked beans with a masher, add a grated onion, a couple garlic cloves, two or three slices of crumbled whole wheat bread, a tablespoon of nutritional yeast, a quarter cup of wheat germ, a scattering of pumpkin or

sunflower seeds, and let's see, what else.... Spices. Well, again, whatever you like. Teaspoon of salt, fresh ground pepper for sure. I'll put in – you should light the barbecue – a teaspoon of basil, of oregano, maybe some sage – grab some sage from the garden, will you? Then you just mash it up well, oh yeah, you

could mix in maybe a tablespoon of oil, the texture should be like this, it should stick together easily, not be too dry or too wet. Squash some into a ball and wheel it around in wheat germ till it's coated, then flatten it out. The patties should be, oh, say half an inch thick, maybe three-and-a-half inches across, give or take.

You should get seven patties of this size and one tiny one. When the barbecue's hot enough, you want to brush a little oil on each patty and cook them, pretty close to the coals, till they turn brown. Maybe five minutes per side? I'll get the cheese and relish. Mustard's a must. You like your buns toasted or plain? Say something. Eat. Sneeze. Punch the wall. Tell me you're bored. Come on, react!

Where on God's green earth are you now?

## Keepers

But I know one day Norbert will come home. That's why I keep his room dusted. That's why every six months I wash his underwear and socks, I air the sheets. I keep the heat off and the door closed to save electricity, also to save the apples – those are Gravensteins, my very favourite. Sometimes when I'm in the hall I hear music from inside, like his clock radio has come on by itself, but when I peep in, all's quiet, all's cold in there.

# Artichoke Hearts

She's a beautiful young streetsmart girl, uh huh, I can't deny that. But look at her, she makes me mad, like she's gonna fall asleep any second, like she's on the verge of a yawn, on her way to noplace with an umbrella. It's depressing.

Here we are, two people in a lounge sharing binoculars. The rain hasn't let up all day. Stupid, I can't understand a girl that dumb. Well, maybe. So many ways to look seductive. What d'you think, you think she'll break? No one's stopping. I like chokes, sometimes I eat a whole jar myself, drink the oil, mmmm, it's quite messy, here open wide let me push this in, oops, try again.

You find her attractive, go ahead admit it, it's OK, lots of ways to show affection. But that's what it isn't, and you do, don't you? It's killer lust. Pass me your binoculars. Ah, look at all those idiots. Notice how anxious folks in cars look. Downtown traffic, crazy noise, never get clear of it. Last two nights I dreamed I was naked from the waist down in public and it was awful, this part here, the big behind. God. Put on a merry widow, halter top, fishnet, stick lips, heels. And they see everything, no matter how fast they're going, those guys behind the wheel with their steely eyes, Rushmore profiles.

Imagine you're a girl on the street, watching, inside every car a possible ride. So many ways to get killed, I guess. I can talk like this because we're buddies, in the same bizz, and I'm a tad fat, right? A tad the wrong body type, a tad swarthy, a tad crude. You're too polite to say, and there I go I've scared you again, you're a sensitive soul – you want to cheer me up (and you do!) and I just scare you. Bye-bye, jock. (I'm kidding!) One more heart for the road. Gee whiz, sounds like a country and western number!

# Bubble and Squeak

I had a thing, like a man's, maybe I was a man, maybe it was a real thing, I'm not sure, but I kept poking it at people, kind of funny, rubbery, and it tickled so much I woke up laughing.

I am tall, oh so slender. I have incredibly wide hips, but a wasp waist and neat breasts. *Encore*! I am young and gorgeous.

Like a crazy ballet, and I was scared for everyone, but in a way it was fascinating, skinned animals flapping through the air.

I stare at the child's face and say, How pretty! And she says this, she says, The moment occurs when you're not consciously looking for it. She says, Spontaneous concentration, not deliberate concentration, brings contact with the environment.

When I fucked this dude with the dirty T-shirt and the gold earring I heard little kids whispering so I kept twisting my head all round till I was dizzy and I saw lots of animals crowded on top of one another against the walls in the corners everyplace.

I was naked from the waist down in public and it was awful, this part here, the big behind. God.

They're finding her again. Divers keep finding her in the lake. She's dead. Always dead. Always pregnant. But the baby's alive. Comes out of her alive. They must be hidden. These water babies.

When I creep up behind him, he jumps in the air, really stunned, old lardface never gets the girl he wants, I see all his molars.

I was on a huge beach full of pavilions, covered fairgrounds, gymnasiums, seedy bars, at a kind of impromptu group therapy session, arguing with this guy, this real macho jerk, about feminism, and it turned out he was really a woman, true bull dyke, and she was so turned on by me, she said, so turned on.

One of those hot perfect days in a cafe. I'm wearing a quiet grey suit and have brushed my hair loose over my shoulders. I'm in love. My face burns – not from wine or the sun, but from happiness.

# HEART

## *Heart*

I hope this is a social visit, I hope this visit will be repeated, I hope I'm on your list of close friends? No, I know. It's my dreams. Well, I'll have to disappoint you. True I've been keeping a journal, but I don't want anyone to see it. At night I read my dreams and they put me to sleep; in the morning I write down new ones, yes I do, fun! Ha ha. But really. Did you watch *Sunset Boulevard* the other evening? The way at the end you find out the corpse has told his story from underwater? That's what I like, some corpse telling you what's happening all the way through. I love Gloria Swanson. The scene where she goes back to the studio and all her old friends flock round, so beautiful, so sad.

# *Gazpacho*

Not my place to infer your state of mind, but I have a sense of when a body needs fussing with, needs some attention. I'd guess it's not really time you're after but a kind of zero, a kind of emptiness that is doing the dishes, mowing the lawn. You look up and notice the sky, the cloud pattern, first time in how long? Hey, maybe you should spend some minutes every day looking at that sky, but there's always too much to do, such a lot of sky.

One thing I do is have these fantasies where I'm really fighting for my life and all the important people are fleas. I lie in bed at night and imagine swimming an ocean in winter, pulling myself forward with strong even strokes through freezing water. Over the waves is Max, tiny on the far shore, waving, flapping his arms, a total gumby. Clarissa and Barb and Pete just dots in the window of a cottage on a hill. Don't even care if it's goodbye or hello.

To be perfectly frank it's forgetting not emptiness I mean. You have that look, kind of psycho-desperate. Correct me if I'm wrong. And me, I'm on a roll, things are pretty good, I've tightened my grip. Go ahead, tell me why you spend so much time heating things up, why at mealtimes you taste nothing.

I say you gotta circulate happiness, document your own, get people to sign up, write happy letters. We need a Royal Commission on despair, need a court injunction to stop hopelessness. Gotta petition for time. Gotta mass market some cold tide deep and rushing that sends a body to sleep giggling.

## *Polenta*

I don't know how to say what I feel, it sounds phony every time I try, I'm not plain empty, I'm not stupid, it's just well nothing has edges, everything's soft, kind of blurry. Sometimes I think I'm a liar. If I'm a liar then these are lies. I'm maybe nervous, but soon as I say it it changes into another feeling. Fear maybe. Imagine a hole as deep as an office building is high filled with down, imagine jumping in, a kind of yellow suicide – anyhow, I watch real careful, I'm looking out for myself. One thing's sure, I figure I'm in for a hard time, not a long time. I don't want to change nothing. I don't think that's right. Worn-out stuff breaks easy. Let people get on with their jobs.

# Wild Rice

One night, a night as strange and still as my wedding night, I'm walking along the beach. My toe hurts. An Indian boy in tiger shorts, tank top and tennis shoes, is doing deep knee bends near the foam. A silver baton stuck in the hard sand beside him. He flexes his biceps, cracks his knuckles, switches on the ghetto-blaster at his feet. He marches on the spot, twirling the baton. The march slows to Tai Chi; he hooks the wand to his belt. Rain begins to fall. I limp to the road. After a while I turn round. He's right there, dancing toward me from streetlight to streetlight and I can't move. No one else in sight, no one to ask what he's doing. He places his music on the sidewalk, then cartwheels fast down the middle of the road. Right in front of me now, he unhooks his baton, tosses it high in the air. I smell his sweat. He is a child, his upturned face close to my face shines with rain.

# Rack of Lamb

I feel guilty all the time, I haven't done anything wrong, leastways nothing particular – no commandments broken, no one hurt bad physically or mentally, everybody thinks I'm a nice person. Yet I have this nervous guilty feeling, as if I'm not doing something I should, or doing something I shouldn't. You probably don't know what I'm talking about. Sometimes I wake up mornings dreaming of eggs and bacon (so help me I'm hungry every minute of the day), but no no no, I gotta work some before I eat, if I eat too much I get fat. The guilt's not so simple, I don't know where it comes from and I don't know what it does. Makes me work like crazy. I feel guilty because I'm always starving, because my fridge is full while others' are empty, because I'm alone with a loaded fridge. Shouldn't keep a loaded fridge around, pardner.

Ever think how fridges are like phones? I always open one or the other when I get so overcome by guilt that I can't even look out the window. The fridge is a real cluttered mess, I never arrange my food properly, a shelf for this a shelf for that, tall stuff at the back, short things at the front. Lettuce in the crisper. Meat in the drawer that says meat. Never. I don't have my numbers organized either, they're pencilled on the wall above the phone. So it's numbers or food, me standing there stunned, listening to the guy who says Please hang up now or the drip of the freezer section beginning to defrost. And no no no, gotta work some more before dialing. Invite my friends over to help in the garden, they all live in apartments and enjoy coming here and digging or building a fence or fixing the chicken coop, whatever. I cook up something special, order in a raft of beer. If it's one friend we just sit at the kitchen table with cake and coffee and talk of guilt. Everyone feels some guilt, nobody knows much about it, so it makes good conversation. Evening comes we play gin rummy, the two of us, drink rum hot in winter with coke in summer and play rummy. Till I say

I gotta go to bed, full day tomorrow, because I hate to think of a person staying late because they feel sorry for me. And she says or he says, Wow I didn't realize it was that time! And I say, Me either well good night so-and-so. Good night yourself and so long. Then I try not to think or eat between when I brush my teeth and when I go to bed, try not to feel let down. It's difficult, because I'm hungry, and no one to say I can't turn on all the lights in the house and have me a feast. No one to explain what I've done wrong, what I've not done.

## Ragout

I regret not visiting my dad more often, not wishing him well before he died. I regret speaking my mind the times I did visit. I regret talking about regrets. I regret having had no children of my own. I regret all this living with Charlie, he has no respect. I regret climbing the hill so many times in heels, ruining my back. I regret not starting over. Ah! Kittens in my lap. I told Charlie about my regrets, and he made me call the travel agency and cancel our trip to Reno. I'm sorry, Charlie. I regret talking to Charlie. I regret Reno. This chair is the wrong colour. I'm sorry now I didn't get red. The wood feels soft in my hand, like warm green plasticine. I regret I didn't water the rubber plant. I'm sorry Charlie didn't run off with that Audrey. I regret worrying so much about nothing, it gave me an ulcer which I regret. Now I can't eat anything I like. I'll never again taste fish au gratin, French stew or pigs in blankets.

# *Trifle*

I woke happy incredibly amazingly happy ecstatic in the dark and wanted to share it. I hurried from bed in the middle of the night, I tried to reach you, but the number I dialed connected me to clanging bells, a whir and a click; when I replaced the receiver, the phone rang; when I picked it up, I heard chimes. I had a feeling of great distance: the bells, the busy signal. Now I can't remember what I wanted to say, I've just got the echo, how I wanted to describe such a complete happiness.

This morning as I ground coffee I thought at length about the implications of my experience. I repeated *flux* several times. *Loss*, too. Flux. Flux. Flux. Flux. Loss. Loss. Loss. Between mouthfuls of sherry-soaked cake remnants.

My intention – to comfort you – sounds presumptuous when I say it. The need hasn't short-circuited, but has grown large and fuzzy. I still want to reassure you in some way help you, but how? With the usual claptrap of a soul in the afterglow of mystical flux? I wasn't going to call till I realized I still had your trifle bowl, when would you want it back, should I bring it over?

No, life has no meaning. I washed the glass bowl and left for work thinking how pretty goldfish would look swimming there. On the highway I went over the actual dream: you and I in an arctic place, above the treeline, in a flat landscape where the sun always shines because it's high summer, July.

# Mystery Meat

I am nervous with fear. I am stupid with rage. I'm close to thirty-five and if life were a day mine would be at noon, when the sun sits overhead. Has fury always been as close as it feels now? I don't understand this speed, this claustrophobia, my own anger that shakes the car. Peter and Alan will fly three thousand miles to go fishing with Peter's father. I've planned my week. I'm going to work hard in the garden. This morning I tied up the daffodils. I'm driving a highway at night toward the airport, straining my eyes to see beyond the headlights, listening to wiper rhythms, hissing rubber. Beside me, Alan's face streams with jelly shadows from rain on the windshield. Be there soon, Mom? Soon as soon, I say. Here we are, bombing along, ninety miles an hour, me gnashing my teeth, Peter in the back seat snoring. Soon as soon as soon? Alan yells. Shh! You'll wake your father.

A semi-trailer plunges through a great pool on the road, a wave gathers, shatters against our windows. Christ! Peter murmurs. Wow! says Alan. I hold the car to its lane, glancing sideways: my son sits enthralled, his face, lit by the lights of oncoming traffic, liquid, incredulous. I guess somewhere the sun moves, because now I feel empty, still, close to the earth, I guess every woman spends life keeping away horror. On Alan's first airplane the flight attendant will serve cold cuts, Alan and Peter will watch farms and cities slip by, they won't be afraid, they will doze, they will work the puzzles I bought.

# *Air*

This room I love, the view's always different, I mean the lake. I don't want to see friends, I don't want to be with other people, to go out at all, not because I'm scared, but because it's cool here, I leave the door open. And because I never turn on a light or even watch TV after dark I don't get bugs with my evening air.

Tonight it looks dangerous, the lake, I guess because people have drowned. I don't like it to change that way, change just because of something I know, not because it *is* different. I don't want it bigger or deeper either, I don't want that economic kind of change, I don't want deer paths and roads underwater, trees with roots locked underground, holding their breath for years.

Thing is I can't help imagining the old logging camp, pike lying low while schools of good guys come dancing through, come hunting fly through the last light, blue-veined dragonfly wing the ideal flag, the dash and gobble worth dying for. Makes my spine tingle. The flooding. Like a queenless roar – listen.

## Seven Treasure Chicken

I smoke when I'm waiting and when I can I drink too. I smoke and I drink to distract myself from worrying about the thing I'm waiting for, because there's always the possibility of the dreadful. My lungs full of smoke and my liver raw, I try to put myself in the way of some bit of lonesome life. I blaze my way to the throne, squat and pee, then eat toast and marg in the kitchen (*What am I waiting for so passionately?*), wishing I had some cheese, a piece of fish. The answer is not bloody TV, boiling water, my own foot tapping. Maybe the wind in the ratty morning glory? I open my purse, fan my credit cards, grin fiendishly across the tips of my fingers. The answer is sleep. No it isn't. So I go out of the house.

Strange outside, because I'm drunk, because I haven't eaten much. Everyone goes up and down. An ordinary man at a bus stop smokes a cigarette, at least he knows what he's waiting for, knows a destination, home with a toilet and kettle no doubt. He's smiling at empty cars. They are still, those empty cars. I'm jostled by a pickpocket, but I'm talking loud and he leaps back shocked. It's all just like on the big screen. It is like a cartoon merry-go-round. Like black and white. I jump the green cat's eyes one by one down the middle of the road, six big strides between each, while round me cars hug the curb each side of the line, windshield faces yell stupid old cunt. Strange outside, because I'm drunk, because I haven't eaten much. Everyone goes up and down.

## *Pansy*

Things is bad bad when you can't look round and see a friend who ain't in a mess whose relationship business health ain't goin to the dogs who ain't lonely gettin fat losin weight scared to death hurtin everybody they love always goin away callin it quits gripin they can't take it no more can't sleep don't want to eat

Yep this ain't everything but it makes history go on have a drink dad it's water a pill ma it's vitamins get rolled it's massage so good for you honey to sweat sweat you're down but you ain't dead yet come home babe have a pansy sandwich turn on all the lights

## Minute Rice

D'you ever wish life was like a fairy tale? I mean you're little again and every day takes you deeper into some forest, you can't feel anything but excitement, and you know even if awful things happen that sooner or later you get to live happily ever after. And as the girl in the story drops crumbs, white stones or locks of her hair, you take stock of the room you're in, the meal you prepared, the wallpaper you chose, the herbs you planted, the kid you nursed, and say, Yep, nod your head and think maybe one day you'll follow this trail, try to get back to where you started and start again, leave a better trail next time, one that can be tracked at a glance, one that leads easily out of the forest, lets you take your bearings, retrace your steps, all in the course of a day, you could be under clear skies by sundown as if you'd never left, you wouldn't have to give anything up.

# HERMITS

## *Hermits*

You know what my mom says? My mom says you're building a ark like in the Bible and when they start flooding us out you're gonna save everyone you like in the ark, you're gonna collect all the animals and all the kids and all the moms, but you'll let the dads drown, because you don't like them. And you'll drive the boat yourself, you're gonna drive right over the dads in the water, you won't let them swim to the land. I don't think that's fair. Even if you're a worker I think people won't let you do that. My dad thinks you don't have the guts and I especially don't want him to drown. He told my mom you are pussywhipped and she said that's not very nice, well I don't think that's very nice. Maybe no one wants to be saved just because you say so, my dad says you're not much better than the people who don't want a big lake and anyway we'll have a lake so big you won't be able to see the other side, and where's your wood anyhow, you got to cut a lot of trees to make a ark, where's your animals and moms, you keep them in cages maybe, keep them in cages in your basement?

When I grow up I'm gonna be a mom and have twelve kids, maybe when I'm twenty, but before that I'm gonna be a small engine mechanic like my dad. Did you know girls can do that now? I'm gonna wear coveralls and get dirty and fix everyone's car. I'll fix your car if you like and charge you hardly nothing, but I won't if you don't save my dad. Course I don't believe they'll let you build a ark, but if they do, or if you build it in your basement where no one can see, then I won't fix your car even if it breaks down real bad, and I won't let anyone else fix it either, I can make the union not let anyone fix it and it'll be broken for good. So if you want a car you better not save anyone, maybe you better stay in your basement and have a train set like Mr Travis. You can paint little trees and make houses, and let the train ride under mountains and over rivers of real water. Once our class went to his place and he took us to his garage to see the train and he let me work it. It's pretty cool, there's special boards to walk on, you look down and feel like a giant. Rails go right through the garage, all over. One train even makes smoke. My dad keeps rabbits in our basement, but they're for eating so we can't give them names, we can't pet them too much. Mr Travis's trains all have names, he talks to them. Mrs Travis brought us a hermit each, but Mr Travis made us eat them outside.

# 1980 Cherry Pie

That phone never stops. I'm not complaining. When I signal, go push the doorbell so I can hang up. I'd rather talk to you than her. Makes me blow through my nose like a dolphin when I think she'll die, sometime soon, die and leave me money. The family thinks I'm snorting when I blow like that, but I'm not. It's kind of a grit teeth sigh, from the diaphragm. A quick pain down there. She's a dear soul. I don't want her money. She worries me. She's not sleeping well. Her windows need cleaning. God knows what's at the bottom of her freezer.

# Rye

My mom lives in Winnipeg, she's cool, she's funny. She gets off the bus in her old Reeboks, looks sixteen. Hey, mom, got a whitey boyfriend? She give me shit, all right, only one who can.

Look at me, man, purer than pure, blonde as snow, yeah? Wrong. I'm black. My foster family are real dark Puerto Rican and I hate whites almost as much as I hate tricks. I never let a trick kiss me, man. That makes them rowdy sometimes, but OK, they get it done faster, plus they don't hang around. I drink some rye, treat them like the assholes they are, and guess what? they get real horny, call me all kinds of trash. What a joke.

My family are Puerto Rican, but not racist like me. They took me in even before they figured my true colour. Me, I was pregnant a few months back, lost the baby in Vancouver, some jerk nearly killed me, and you know, they found out in Winnipeg, in Edmonton, in Calgary, even Toronto, for Christ's sake – I get phonecalls from girls in all those places. There's sluts in the business, sure, but there's sisters and they know me. Maybe they're all not so racist, not so full of hate as I am, but then they *look* black.

Larry been playing bingo a lot, sometimes like five or six hours straight. I don't know, he's getting bored with this city. He's a nice guy mostly, he treats me better than some treat their girls. I'll stay for the summer I guess, the Nadine thing shook me. She looked awful when they dragged her out the lake. Larry and me, we may go south in the fall. The guy who did Nadine still walking around. Tricks like that always horny, soon as they come they're horny again. Horny and cheap. You got to feed them enough rye, treat them like shit, get a cabbie to come back in an hour take them away or they'll want to screw all night for a hundred, maybe threaten you with a gun or a knife, then waste you if they're really crazy.

## Crumbs

I want these surfaces clean!

# Sesame

More than anything in the world now, I want that little girl to love me. I don't see why she has to live with her dad. He thinks he's so educated, thinks he's God controlling the universe, he makes her eat with chopsticks, scares her with *Arabian Nights*. If she came back I know we could manage fine – long as he left us alone. When I was her age my mom told me that the specks in a girl's navel were the seeds of the children she would have, so I used to open my shirt behind the holly hedge, crumble soil in. If she wants an ice cream I say yes, or I say no – if she's been good, if she's been bad. Sometimes I don't even cook her favourite things. If she's been very bad I make her eat Brussels sprouts, they're good for her. I'd never tell her the belly button story.

# Salt

Know what my husband said to me the other day? The problem with you is I only want to make love to you when I'm not horny. When I'm horny I only want to make love to other women. And he must've been chewing on this a long time because it's the first thing other than pass the salt he's said in more than a month. Figure it out, he said, when I asked him what he meant. So I've been figuring. And I figure he cares for me like I care for him, a lot. I figure he wants to be gentle with me and not imagine I'm some movie star. That's why he's down to drinking just two evenings in the week. What we do together is Friday afternoons grocery shop, then beer and fish and chips at the pub. He loves tomato juice in his beer. Sometimes I get a twinge of guilt because he doesn't know I have a special friend. As a matter of fact my special friend doesn't know I have another friend, an old friend, special in a different way – a good dancer, we like to dance together.

Practice deceit is a good way to put it: it's easy to lie when you do it all the time. It was easy when my friend lived here. Now he lives far away it's hard, I have to invent a reason for a long trip every couple of months, instead of telling little lies every week. It's difficult to make up a big story, I prefer lots of little ones. My friend's got gypsy blood, he changes towns pretty often. Why would I go to some little mining town in the mountains? Why? Why would I go camping in Alberta in January, 40 below? Why would I return with a camera full of pictures of me?

Interesting what my husband said about other women and being horny, it makes sense. Because you know, I see lust on his face, well, it makes me laugh or makes me sad or makes me nervous, but with my special friend and my dancing friend, it's OK, guess I'm an 'other' woman, I get caught up in that crazy passion.

# Girl Guide Cookies

My granddaughter's only concern is that her cookies are sold, she has two big boxes and we've been going mall to mall, the three of us, three generations.

In the creation of mountains some morbid air is displaced, my daughter says. I don't know what she's talking about. That's not highfalutin, she says, that's a fact. She read it in *Mysteries of the Unknown*. The bad air kind of infiltrates a town, say, and weird things start to happen. Maybe the hens go broody, the water starts to stink, or all the men begin collecting those little plastic jam containers you get in restaurants. Things you might not connect unless you knew about the mountain stuff. She says Atlantis was a country flooded by the sea. I think she's just nervous and upset, all this selling cookies, losing her husband. I guess we're all on edge. At the Bay my granddaughter asked some Hindu drivers who were playing cards on the hood of a cab if they'd seen her father. She asked three sailors sitting at a bus shelter eating pizza. They were nice, my granddaughter played up to them and they all bought cookies.

Suddenly I'm remembering a jug of flowers on the sideboard at home. Bluebells you put in a vase make shepherd's crooks, they wilt then perk up again. Blue fades paler and paler to off-white.

I went into 7-11 and bought sour-cream-and-onion potato chips and a coke. My granddaughter says the chips are raunchy. We smell them, and yes, they are bad. She doesn't want a cookie, so she's allowed to buy a chocolate bar. Bees swarming for no reason, my daughter says, is another strange mystery caused by shifting mountains.

## Summer Ice

My face feels bruised, shattered, wet. Full of gravel. I'm slumped against a mesh fence enclosing tennis courts, in the shadow of a huge tree. Here I am, bearing the pain, the big accident I've been rehearsing for, just sitting quietly in the shade on a July afternoon. Tell my heart to keep beating, tell my heart to do its worst. The free end of a garden hose waving in the air, filling the street with sparkling voices, kids' voices, now isn't that silly?

In winter find a silver box on the back door step. Remember a lover's pale lips. D'you worry about change? Change in yourself, changes in the way you feel about things or people? Grip the chill box, gift box, stroke its gleaming surface, sharp edges. Little girls in the street take turns jumping on a frozen puddle, trying to break the ice. It doesn't matter, darling. You and I sit on large circular chairs obliquely facing each other; frost patterns glint from the carpet. I can't look at you. Yep, it's an expensive box, pretty design. Climb shivering from bed in the middle of the night. God, can't get warm! Look at me, I've had a life of accidents. Plump middle-aged woman holding her aching head under the sun. Take a fresh look round. No use now, no need. Remember why girls would try to break ice.

## Peas

Mum died of a shrug. Give me a drag of your cigarette. It wasn't really funny, the way her shoulders came up as if to say, We're all in God's hands, what can be done? Put your arm round me. Sol is playing soldier again, he's into demolition these days. Nice explosion, kid. I know I shouldn't be smoking, but what the hell. You humour a person when you're feeling hopeless, I tried with seeds and dirt, but he upended the pots, said they were rocket launchers, stood transformers on top of the dirt, spat sweet peas at them through a McDonald's straw till they fell off. I want to put my faith in God, I want to rejoice, some kind of rebirth, not like on TV, for real, I'd be strong and certain of something.

Mum looked peaceful. I knew she wasn't quiet in her mind. Sol is OK, he curls up like that sometimes for minutes, tight as a ball, soon he'll leap, he'll burst, arms and legs and fingers flying.

## Sizzlers

Inside the yellow pepper I found five baby green peppers. Look! See how perfect the yellow skin, the green five babies in their yellow house? They don't know what worry is. They don't know who they are. Remember I used to read at night in front of the TV? Now I have to stay by the window with the news under my nose.

And it's always the murder scene, the murder scene, the murder. It's wrong to ask who is to blame. We must be hopeful. When I am hopeful, the future looks beautiful, I question nothing. Mom and Dad and Mom's brother Alec will soon arrive in the family Ford.

Mother taught us how to tat, now I do it on the bus. People are interested, they've never seen it before. I give them my number, say I will teach them tatting. I pretend I've been married. Since my husband died, I say when they ask, since my husband died.

Look at the headlines, child abuse terrorist crash hostage freed drugs super sizzlers. I tat my flowers on folded heavy paper. To fill in the picture I cut vases from Christmas paper and little tables from advertisements. In my mind's light I expect the family Ford, don't you? Hold a finger in front of your eye and see its ghost. Look right through the ghost, right through the open window to the highway.

# Butter

My mother's in there now using womanly wiles on my dad. So he'll think it's his idea to ask me if I want to store my stuff in his garage. She says she's known him forty years. Pretty soon he'll come out and ask me and I'll say yes, if it's not too much trouble, storing my stuff in the garage will be very convenient.

Thing is I'll know that he knows that I know he knows my mother's been using her wiles, that's the way things are done at our house, always have been. I used to think Mother was controller, then when I got a little older I decided she was least in control – after all, Dad's known her forty years too – but now I'm not so sure. Yesterday she wanted more light and today I watched him knock a hole in the wall for another window in the kitchen. Maybe what it amounts to is a simple question a simple response in their private language. Here he comes now, looking serious, working his hands. Mom's at the window smiling, winking.

# *Wishbone*

I said, D'you find my face attractive? And the doctor said, Sure. And I said, So why shouldn't my body match my face? And he said, Talk to the nutritionist. And I said, You think I haven't tried a hundred diets? And he said, I don't want you to rush into this.

I'd like that planter lifted out, moved over by the house. Ben and I started to do it last year, but we found two salamanders underneath and I didn't want to disturb their home, so we dropped the box back in. Maybe crushed them. We hadn't meant to drop it. The thing's so damned heavy. I didn't want to look. At any rate they're bound to be gone by now. If you take one end, I'll take the other. One, two, three! God, the bottom's rotten. Will it hold, d'you think? Keep lifting. There's a nice fat worm.

So I said, You'll get paid. And he said, It's nothing to do with money. I said, Why then? Why should you control the way I look? And he didn't know what to say. I said, I'll go to the States. Holy cow, it's a tail, they still live here. Can you see them? Oh, never mind the box, dump it anywhere. Aren't they cute? See their tiny tiny hands. How do they manage to survive in such a narrow space. They must come out at night to do their hunting. What do they eat anyway?

Look, they're wiggling behind that stone, both together, they're just like human couples. What shall we do, we can't put the planter back. Perhaps you could make a box, could you? A little house we could bury in the hole. Use one of the sides of the planter. They'll think it familiar wood. Couple of nails, you could do it in a jiffy, you're clever with your hands. I'll clean up while you work. Just a quick box for the salamanders, then I'll shovel in dirt.

You should make a little chimney, so they can breathe, so they can get out, at night, to hunt. I'll plant lobelia over them, trailing lobelia, blue cloud white stars. I wonder how long they've been here, if they've had families.

It's a simple operation, no side effects. It's called gastric staple. The stomach can hold only half a cup of food after surgery. I know I'm not really huge, but I want to do something before I'm an elephant. Now that I'm single again.

They are like people aren't they? People who live together a long time. These guys play it cool. Think how they must feel, their house wrenched from its foundations as they sleep, nowhere to hide.

## Melting Moments

I've been hugging a lot of people lately, mostly other women, and they're all different, the way your arms go round changes every time. I always thought the human body a simple arrangement – head bone connected to the neck bone, that sort of thing – but now I realize it's complicated. Sometimes I hug shoulders, sometimes waists, sometimes ribs, sometimes even hips. Different height, different build. Some bodies are hard, others soft, some pliant, some stiff. Flesh kind of floats on some, on others it seems attached to the bone. Also how the person hugs back, if they do. I myself reach round and go for the spine, dig my fingers in there, like a fire fighter at a pole. There are people who kiss necks, who graze cheeks, who frisk ribs, who say Ah, or Ooo, or Oh dear. A bear hug can last a split second, leave you giggling; a limp hug can last hours and sap all your strength. Also if you're giving or receiving. I had a hug last week, let me say.

I said what I always say to a friend who seems like she's in a really bad way: Don't worry about your kids, you can learn to cope with anything, after all they haven't killed anybody. And it turns out the woman's son is in jail waiting to go to court on a murder charge. We stood there in my living room, she and her husband and I and we put arms round each other and wept. We just hugged, broke away, hugged, set each other off and couldn't quit.

## Coriander

Chinese parsley. Sexual frustration. Weekends he wants to buy a compact disc player, silly man. We're very happy together. He bought me a hat to shade my face from the sun, he's afraid of skin cancer. Cilantro. On Sunday the men in the neighbourhood get together and stand round looking forceful and talk about the cost of nuts and bolts. He's got about five thousand records he never plays. I can't imagine going through a separation, so many do these days, hunting out another partner. I bought him a security engraver because I'm afraid of break and entry. Chinese parsley. Cilantro. Music recorded digitally, he explains, is notes coded – numbers to be decoded by a laser, reproducing the music in the privacy of your own home. We're pretty happy despite the fact I'm getting kind of fat. Sunday afternoons is our passion time. Rest of the week he's meek and mild, says he'll wait a while till the prices drop or something even better is invented.

# Cocktails

I guess they'll have a job dragging the next murder, once they flood the valley. It's amazing, everyone's informed, we all know it's a drink we drink to get drunk, pimento olive at the bttom.

Flooding the valley will turn town upside down. We talk employment, growth, big bucks. What about animals, trees...? Want mine? I can't finish, I've had two already, they go to my head.

I could do it, you know. You saw me on African night. I'm not bad in make-up, n'est-ce pas? not too bad in a slinky gown? I'll toast you a toast, I'll drink to whatever you all believe in.

Elixir. Made from wormwood and gin, the housewife's proven aphrodisiac. So you think they'll really build a dam? Darling, you want to make a small wager, under the table, so to speak? I've got a theory.

Fix the man a molotov cocktail, won't he like that fine? I'm drunk. Hearings, he said, public council meetings. Dreaming. This many brimming cut-glass heirlooms, imagine, left to evaporate.

I live here. House and home, I pay taxes. I'm a commuter. I had a flat one morning last week. Fixed it myself, no problem. Just out of curiosity, what about you? You ever think it might be suicide?

With orange bitters, that's the sophisticated way. Ah, to wake up into one massive communal belly-roiling hangover. More gin, I like 'em dry – like James Bond's women, decent by half an inch.

## Capers

I know I'm lying in the bath, but that's what you're seeing, not what I'm seeing, let me tell you what I see, first let me say I like what I'm seeing better than I like what I'm hearing, stop eating almonds, I'm seeing red poppies, double red poppies, the kind called by a girl's name, what I might call my daughter if I had one, in a pickle jar on the window sill and the petals are falling, big red petals, onto the sill or onto the carpet by the toilet, then beyond the poppies the sky, the blue morning sky, then tracer fire though I've never seen tracer fire just heard people who lived through air raids talk about tracer fire, on the sky like tracers is water going up, it's the sprinkler, the spray catches the sun every few seconds, a silver crackling in the sky outside the poppies, and I'm thinking, listen what I'm thinking.

My body looks pale and dead underwater, the water hides nothing from your eyes. Last night when you tickled me I wasn't enjoying it, I didn't want sex, I lied when I said I did, I wanted to scratch. We're silly to think each house contains a mystery, each room a secret, each body a conspiracy. We gobble secrets, fill our mouths, and they dissolve leaving only a sweet hollow taste.

## Food Food

Lemur hugging lemur on a branch in *National Geographic* Africa
The Waiting Room. I miss my back teeth when I brush, the den-
tist hurts my gums, I swim through his big nocturnal eyes and
grunt.

You all right? he says. Yes. Sure. I was falling asleep. That's good,
he says. He shows me food he's scraped from my molars. You
must be careful. Small food, colourless, paste in fact, shameful.

Outside, sky beats on my car; driving, I feel rested and clean and
relieved and hungry for a grilled cheese sandwich, fries, vanilla
shake. Desire jolts me: at a stop light a ridiculous muscle man
brushes my hood with his beefy palm; again I forget and again
remember *indri indri*, behold, behold – what the natives told the
white man, pointing.

# *World*

In the morning everyone goes up and down, in the afternoon they go side to side, it's what I've come to realize. In Canada it's whiskey and cornbread in winter, kedgeree here on the West Coast; Caesar salad, nachos, fuzzy navels on summer evenings. At night couples go hump to sleep, singles make like macaroni, girls and boys work at buck teeth. Just before dawn all bloat with solemn idiotic stories, and sink, spinning millwheels run out of grist. Even the all-night cafes in the city beyond the valley are suddenly still, laughter finished; mouths forget to close, waitresses slump over swamp cloths. Even the murderers ... but I won't go into that. Even the animals. Right now all the people alive in the world are alive but some are dead now. Of all the dead people in the world, some are remembered, some so well that they seem to live. Most dead are completely completely forgotten. Right now all the people alive in the world are invisible to me. No, through the front window I see the head of a little girl gliding past the fence. She's happy, I take it, not starving not in pain. I can think of, I can summon all the people alive, there they are in my head, a great multitude. The finch is easier, here in the sunshine in his cage on the porch of my house in the world. Can I say the window eats the world? the frame makes me feel safe? the glass I look through is the forgotten dead? I'm making like macaroni and it's not even night. But that's stupid. The girl glides by again, head and shoulders above the fence. I'm a weak person, not doing enough. They should put me and every other single in a great vat of boiling water, soften our hearts. All the couples in the world are singles. I want you to stop listening to me. Put your eyes (imagine) on the most distant possible object. If it's night where you are and dark, not too far north or south and you are in some room with curtains drawn, you will be close enough to walk over and touch what you see. Listen. Someone is breathing, someone is eating, someone is buying. You can only touch stars with numbers. I bet you can hear your own belly full of food. Let me tell you what I think. I think we must put everything on the surface, a complicated job, we must be very careful, we must remember.

# Rolls

Have you ever noticed what happens between when you've finished cooking and when you start eating? There's a gap. Usually you hardly realize, especially when you have company or a big family and cooking seems to blur into eating, but there's an interval.

That's the time you set the table, put out salt and pepper, butter, whatever else goes with the meal. This is a bridge over the twilight zone. You get a twinge of sadness, putting things in serving dishes, crossing from the kitchen to the dining room. You are lost, you lose everything. This is the moment everything familiar becomes unfamiliar, or maybe you fool yourself and you really are at home on this bridge and recognize everything. At least, when you sit down with guests or family you're OK again.

The same thing happens to me at hellos and goodbyes, when it's the most natural thing in the world to hug a person. Hugging changes everything and I'm lost again, I lose everything, I close my eyes. And hug. In my mind it's like a breeze over water, tilting sheets of light, like summer everywhere and everywhere a door opening, when I hug like that, hanging onto a body. I hug everyone in sight. Assembly line hugs. A fit of hugging. Gone mad with hugging. Make it last, don't want to let go, I belong here!

# Debt

Here I sit sound and safe, wearing my cardigan and my patient supercilious nervous smile, the vegetarian at room temperature, the vegetarian at home. A pile of unpaid bills on the table. I won't go to any more weddings or christenings, nobody to force me. How could the family survive? I'm starving, I want to swindle the government. No kids for me, I won't be any man's fruitful vine. I'm so hungry I could eat my shoe.

I'll make a way of speaking. Trust him. Share him. Thank him. Communicate. I'll undermine the question before I'm clever enough to ask it. *The patriarchal system.* Give. Inflict. Build. Obey. Daddy gave me a tomato and told me not to eat daddy was talking talking I heard him it was amazing the words I didn't know they were words now I do they were sounds coming from his mouth he said this is a tomato when mother said yes daddy's lips didn't move it was wonderful it felt good talking talking though there was guilt I felt guilty all the time it was exciting I could feel the muscle in the talking not my muscle I won every argument against myself in the dictionary I was playing a game sharing the tomato. Satisfy him. Fail him. Discover him. Lose him. Believe him. Succeed. Survive him. Begin.

In the family I was safe, everyone fed me. Journey. Accomplish. Starve him. Cherish him. I watch God's TV, bought with God's money. A man whose smile affects only the corners of his mouth tells me what to believe. Think. Change him. Fashion him. Advertise him. Defeat him. Expect him. Trap him. Force him. Worry him. Please him. Desire him. Exist. Produce him. Prove him. Fear him. Anger him. Buy him. Worship him. He says, Take the 's' off 'goods.' He asks for money. He says, How can the family survive? Behind him I hear canaries in his church. He says, In the blindness came the vision. (Twitter twitter, little smile.) He gives me all the words I must not trust. Trust is number one.

# Pig Wine

Pig wine, pig wine, call the ombudsman, the kids are in the living room decking out the Christmas tree. I watch through the window from the frozen yard and they are strangers. Another way of saying

she's in the book. He's a dream. I don't even know her. He says everything's happening too fast. Her heart gave up. I guess the suspense was too much.

Pig wine, pig wine, call the police, mother's in the bathroom fixing the toilet. The line of my life skates the edge of the storm. Another way of saying

you can read him like a book. She's in a dream. I know him too well. Nothing much happening. His heart's not in it. I guess the boredom is too much.

Pig wine, pig wine, call the brigade, father's in the kitchen fixing the range. Star light star bright, cones in the fireplace turning to ash.

## Venison

Symbols I must not trust include the alphabet. I can't trust any food: who would taste for the King's taster? But I do trust you.

## Lamb

Late at night I scrub the day's dishes and the house reruns the last
mad toothpaste dash; late at night when not only has the world not
whited out blown sky high, not only are my kids tucked safely in
bed and the stickiness is washed from my fingers and all the
rooms wait still at my back while my husband prepares for bed,
checks windows, locks the doors (and I accept the word *husband*),
I let go, I allow the stories my father told to sweep down, clouds
before a storm, sheep on the run; the knives and forks line up, the
dishcloth kisses every surface until all is clear, clean, enough, and
I'm limp as that rag, know I'll sleep.

# Hunger

Shoe lies on the ground. Hey. Man kicks shoe. Swearing man. Drunk man. In a country where everyone speaks with an accent. Shoe floats on the marsh. Woman rescues shoe. Shocked man. Hurt woman. In a place where everyone speaks a different language. Son of a bitch.

## Lobster

The bearded face too close to mine. What is the mouth in the face saying? It doesn't matter. I won't get mad. Are you gonna take me to hospital? Are you gonna save my life? Jesus, the kitchen seems

big – waves behind you as tall as people. Except I know – I even *know* they're not really there. It's a long way from the chair to the door. Please don't touch me, I'll make it in a minute. Are my

eyes open? Both of them? My whole body aches, my fillings ache, teeth feel like electricity. Hard to walk! Weird how near everything is! You've got to look at my fridge. So cold so cold so

cold. Crossing a room is not supposed to work this way. I said don't touch me! Keep still! Is it true my fridge is broken? I can see lights. Sweet Jesus, make him take his filthy hands off me!

# *Jam*

Rain dripping from the house eaves and a grey sky, the dill gone to seed and bowing, tips heavy with white beads. Last daisies sprawled across the baby's breath. I love gazing at fall in the empty garden, remembering the summer in terms of flowers.

Rain in stair rods, in sheets, cats and dogs. I cut resin from a plum, watch myself in the mirror squashing fruit flies. The rain makes me so tired, but I can't sleep in the middle of the day, must wait, I've plums still to pick.

More old men in the pampas gaze through the window at me looking out, we've been doing this all summer. They're soaking wet, I should ask them in by the fire, but I like them there, they like me here.

Rain filling the gutters and overflowing the barrel, mist alternates with needles. Soon I'll put on a coat and go taste the rain, smell it. I'll be a pincushion, my padded shoulders, turn down my hat brim, I've got a charming smile, fill my pockets with soft plums, tell the old men it's rolls of paper dough, and get them to talk to me. Take off my hat and talk to them. Be so cosy.

O Martha Washington geranium, best blooms in the neighbour-hood, eat your soul out, George. Big as the yard, a single plant, flowers so pink and dark-hearted, George would lose himself an election and fifty-two women could win the world when the world lost its head.

What d'you bet I can do it? I'm half-dressed, midriff exposed, a little fat but no one will notice, I'll wear shades and cowboy boots, shove my hands in my pockets, plum skin warm as a baby's bum. I'll open the door, march out of this house, run the driveway and saunter along the road, grab a stalk of grass to chew, stop at the first bar and trade the grass for a yellow plastic sabre cocktail stick to pick my teeth, pick a fight.

All of a sudden I have this vision: I'm the plum princess, I'm in a crowd and everything is glistening, everyone looking as I take off my coat, show my body, and people murmur and applaud, women as well as men, because I'm a woman, and my body is not ugly but smooth, pale, sweet, round, tidy, beautiful.

# Rice

My daughter does this funny thing with her hands when she sees Dave or me after she's not seen us for a while. Dave calls it a microwave because it's fast and almost no movement at all. She keeps her arms stiff at her sides, darts the fingers of both hands quickly away from her body, then back. A tiny swimming motion. A long distance hug. Her eyes showing how happy she is.

I take her to the library and sit her looking at picture books in the children's section. The library's a good place to begin, if you have the time to read. You need a library card and people are nice and helpful. Dave says there are as many murders in the library as on TV, just as many awful things as in the newspaper. He's wrong, there's worse. But I get more afraid in The Brick, buying appliances, than I get by my daughter's side reading horror in articles and books. Nobody tries to snow me, or sell me stuff. I look at her microwave and want to know every terrible thing going on in the world, and if it gets real bad I can always close my book, look over her shoulder into the same old forest.

Air 42
Artichoke Hearts 28

Bubble and Squeak 29
Butter 61

Capers 70
1980 Cherry Pie 51
Cocktails 69
Coffee 24
Coriander 68
Couscous 17
Crumbs 54

Debt 75
Dill Pickles 22

Fiddlehead Greens 12
Food Food 71

Gazpacho 34
Gingerbread 25
Girl Guide Cookies 57

Heart 33
Hermits 49
Hunger 80

Jam 82

Keepers 27
Kibbles 15

Lamb 79
Lemon Loaf 16
Lobster 81

Melting Moments 67
Minute Rice 45
Mystery Meat 41

Onion 20

Pansy 44
Peas 59
Peppers 11
Pig Wine 77
Polenta 35

Rack of Lamb 37
Ragout 39
Rice 84
Roast Duck 18
Rolls 74
Rye 52

Salt 56
Sesame 55
Seven Treasure Chicken 43
Sizzlers 60
Soyburgers 26
Spaghetti Bolognese 23
Summer Ice 58

Tomatoes 13
Trifle 40

Venison 78

Wild Rice 36
Wishbone 65
World 72

Michael Kenyon was born in England, but now lives on North Pender Island, B.C. He has worked as, among other things, a deck hand, a diver and a cab driver, and is on the editorial board of *The Malahat Review*. His work has appeared in *Prism International, Canadian Fiction Magazine, Epoch, Dandelion, Fiddlehead, Descant* and other literary journals. A novel, *Kleinberg*, is forthcoming from Oolichan Books.